YOUR KNOWLEDGE H

- We will publish your bachelor's and master's thesis, essays and papers

- Your own eBook and book - sold worldwide in all relevant shops

- Earn money with each sale

Upload your text at www.GRIN.com and publish for free

Shree Prasad Devkota

Nepal: Ten years Armed Conflict and educational Impact on Children

GRIN Verlag

Bibliografische Information der Deutschen Nationalbibliothek:

Die Deutsche Bibliothek verzeichnet diese Publikation in der Deutschen National-
bibliografie; detaillierte bibliografische Daten sind im Internet über http://dnb.d-
nb.de/ abrufbar.

Imprint:

Copyright © 2014 GRIN Verlag GmbH
Druck und Bindung: Books on Demand GmbH, Norderstedt Germany
ISBN: 978-3-656-67932-5

This book at GRIN:

http://www.grin.com/en/e-book/274904/nepal-ten-years-armed-conflict-and-educa-
tional-impact-on-children

GRIN - Your knowledge has value

Der GRIN Verlag publiziert seit 1998 wissenschaftliche Arbeiten von Studenten, Hochschullehrern und anderen Akademikern als eBook und gedrucktes Buch. Die Verlagswebsite www.grin.com ist die ideale Plattform zur Veröffentlichung von Hausarbeiten, Abschlussarbeiten, wissenschaftlichen Aufsätzen, Dissertationen und Fachbüchern.

Visit us on the internet:

http://www.grin.com/

http://www.facebook.com/grincom

http://www.twitter.com/grin_com

Ten years Armed Conflict and educational Impact on Children

A Research Seminar Paper

Submitted by

Shree Prasad Devkota

School of Education

Kathmandu University

Bal Kumari, Lalitpur

2014

Table of Content

Introduction

The armed conflict started from the year since 1996 to 2006 against the Nepali state by the Maoist party in Nepal. No any Nepalese is free from the conflict and its effect, affected all aspects of livelihood and dominion (Pherali, 2006). The armed conflict in Nepal has left a legacy of some 15,000 dead (INSEC, 2007), and more than 1,300 missing (ICRC, April 2009). According to Shrestha, (2004) he has acknowledged that the armed conflict also destroyed human life and physical infrastructures as well. Similarly, Pherali (2011)states that children from rural people to the urban, being abduct from their home, and killing of innocent children and people, people being homeless, people being internally and externally displaced, the big number of children being orphan and homeless were the regular phenomena in that period. However, ten years armed conflict with the political aim has been the longest ever conflict witness in the past of Nepal. Ten years since then, the conflict has overcome almost 70 out of 75 districts, making it a problem of Nepal in many sectors like health, education etc .Therefore it can be said that Ten years conflict has a profound effect on children development negatively.

Armed conflict and Children Involvement

According to Angucia (2009), the use of children in conflict is perhaps as old as humanity. Moreover children's involvement in warfare ranges from as far back as ancient Greece (Macmillan, 2009) to till now. According to him, children involvement in conflict is mostly in South African countries. Similarly there were heavily children used in ten years armed conflict in Nepalese armed conflict, Shrestha, (2004), which was beyond the child convention and their right. UNICEF (2005) considers childhood to be a period when children are given an opportunity to grow and develop to their full potential. For this, we people have the accountability to provide them safe space to grow, play and develop. Nevertheless,Pauletto&Patel (2010)states that children have been conscripted, kidnapped, pressured, or duped into joining armed groups in conflict and somehow these scenarios was experimented to involve children in armed conflict. But Neupane (2003) disagrees it and claims that the social and political agenda of the Maoists motivated young people and unequal conditions that surrounded them to motivate to involve in armed conflict even they were below 18 years old. Also, many children decide to join armed groups without explicit coercion, although their decisions cannot be regarded as voluntary because they are nearly always bounded by desperation and survival needs, (Wessells, 2002). And in Nepali context, some children were enforced to engross in armed conflict cause of missing their parents by conflict and they have alternative way to stay in society. These conditions enforce them to left their academic career and they involved in armed conflict. Some are recruited as combatants and some were recruited as a cooks, labors and messenger. And most children were killed in armed conflict some were injured, uproot from their homes and communities, internally displaced or refugees, orphaned or separated from their parents and families, Pherali (2011).They were victims of trauma as a result of being exposed to violence, deprived of education and recreation, at risk of becoming conflict victims.

Armed Conflict and Children Education

The conflict that becomes known out of socio-economic and political problem has affected the education sector most, Pherali (2007). In some illustrations, revolutionary party and Government security man have threatened on the pupils and their teachers to support their cause from two sides. Similarly Pyakurel (2006) has stated that rebels have even threatened the school custodians to implement the 'Janavadi Sikchhaya', the Maoists curriculum and stop the government system. If the students and teachers had failed to listen, they also were threatened of their lives or are killed. Alike the Maoist party initially targeted and closed private schools across the country but more recently the Maoists appear willing to tolerate private school, possibly because the schools represent important sources revenue. And according to Sharma and Khadka (2006), the government security men, on the other hand also constantly harassed the teachers and students for supporting the rebels or for sheltering those overnights and providing food to them. Those students and teachers are thus, the losses of the two ideological conflicts. They are sufferers of the conflict, which is fought for supremacy between two military parties (State and Maoist). Education in Nepal is thus, under serious dilemma. Bombs go off, dozens killed, hundreds injured, school closed, exams cancelled and so on make headlines almost every day in media (Thapa & Sijapati, 2004)..So thinking the interplay between education and conflict, we can analyses the nexus of the 'Ten years armed conflict' and education in Nepal and shows how education served indirectly as one of the main causes of the violent conflict.

With extremely large destruction of its infrastructure, education has been badly affected during the moment of ten years armed conflict. According to Shrestha, (2004), both the conflicting parties (State and Maoist) have been using the educational institutions as training centers and army camps. He further states that schools have been closed in many villages, students feared coming to schools. While the Maoist party forces the children &students to join them, the security forces accuse them of being Maoists & assert them from their schools, (The Kathmandu Post, 2004). As a result thousands of children have been deprived of their right to education. And it goes ahead the condition of children's education has been degrading. The children have been deprived of education, been illiterate and have been trapped in the vicious circle of illiteracy, unemployment, poverty. They have not obtained the essential opportunities of physical, mental, moral and overall development through education .UNESCO (2004) states that thousands of orphans (victims from both sides) have seen their parents, siblings, or friends being beaten up or tortured or killed. According to UNESCO report, over 4,000 children have been internally displaced; some of them even live on the street, exposed to various types of danger. Many displaced children have witnessed violence and destruction and thousands have been traumatized themselves. Children who have been directly affected or who have witnessed violence from either side are deeply upset or have developed a sense of revenge and engaged in crime,(Pauletto &Patel, 2010). Lacking protection and guidance, orphaned children have fallen into bad habits, often misbehaving & developing a deep sense of revenge, (Bush &Saltarelli, 2000). Their youth has been stained by cruelty, inhumanity and helplessness. So their growing up in such an environment is certain to have server effect on their psychology which may destruct their present along with future life and it can have severe adverse effects on the society as well.

Post Conflict Situation and Children Reintegration On Education

The Twelve-Point Agreement signed by the Seven-Party Alliance (SPA) and the CPN (Maoist), on 22 November 2005 along with the successive popular peaceful movement of April 2006 brought an end to the armed conflict in Nepal, Pherali (2011) .Notwithstanding the delays, confusions and contradictions among major stakeholders on integration and rehabilitation, ultimately, the major political parties took a historic decision on 1 November 2012 and signed a Seven-Point Agreement on integration and rehabilitation of the former combatants and other armed conflict victims children.

In Uganda, the NGOs and the Commission provide some vocational skills, school fees, help for education, onetime non-food items such as cups, plates, mattresses, for the war victim children(Angucia, 2009). Similarly, some kinds of initiations were done from government,

NGOs, INGOs in Nepal but they were not the long term programs and were only the material base,.In Mozambia, most of the war affected children become trusted and productive adult members of their communities and nation by means of education(Boothby, Crawford, &Halperin, 2006).The reintegration process of Nepal was like the Uganda which was for the short term basis. The war victims were termed as *ladaku* by the government which created them to be self-stigmatized. They felt hesitation as society didn't accept them properly as being *ladaku* and psychologically traumatized. For this, Psycho-social support and awareness, especially in the public sphere. Therefore, psycho-social programs should continue and be expanded according to their need. Dialogue between the different communities and groups that address the fears and needs of their and which encourage genuine listening should be promoted. Because of war, they couldn't continue their education and also they didn't want to continue at the present situation as they have gap to study, Pherali (2011). After the peace process also, the armed conflict affected children felt that they have low and poor academic achievement and felt themselves backward on education so they don't want to continue their study. So in their voices, they have said that they should have other alternatives for secure livelihood.

Conclusions

There are so many laws, policies, plans and adequate space to reintegrate the conflict victim children but the implementation is not seen proper in the case of Nepal. The human rights, child convention and different NGOs, INGOs are focusing on the issues of conflict victims children but the children has become the fire brigade. The voices of the children are heard only after being affected, the precautions were not taken earlier. The programs for the armed conflict victims are only for the short term basis and which would not support them to adjust in the society and for the livelihood (Boothby, Crawford, & Halperin, 2006). The education seems poor and they are not educated well. Because of this, they don't want to continue so other alternative programs are necessary for the armed conflict victim children of Nepal. According to report of ICRC (2009), lack of good education and participation in war, they felt insecure and voiceless in the society and are searching for the helping hands for proper integration. For this the government of Nepal and donors need to commit to increasing funding to all conflict-affected children , at all stages of vulnerability and beyond – in emergencies, chronic crises, early reconstruction and long-term development.

References

Angucia, M. (2009).Children and war in Africa: The crisis continues in Northern Uganda. *International Journal on World Peace, 26* (3), 77-95. Retrieved from http://www.jstor.org/stable/pdfplus/10.2307/20752896.pdf?acceptTC=true

Bhattarai, B.R. (2003). *The political economy of the People's War. In The people's war in Nepal: Left perspectives.* New Delhi: Adroit Publishers.

Boothby, N., Crawford, J., &Halperin, J. (2006). Mozambique child soldier life outcome study: Lessons learned in rehabilitation and reintegration efforts. *Global Public Health, 1*(1), 87-107. Retrieved from https://childprotection.wikischolars.columbia.edu/file/view/Boothby+Crawford+%26+Halperin_Mozambique+Child+Soldiers.pdf

Bush,K. &Saltarelli ,D.(2000) .*The two Faces of Education in Ethnic Conflict: Towards a Peacebuilding Education for Children.*Kathmandu:UNICEFInnocenti Research Centre

Catherine,H.A .,Eduardo,M.,Ngugi, Lynn,N., Tanja,S.,Totland, Thea.,Britt,V.D.H.I.,Rosana,V. &Katja,Z. *(2008). "Protecting the Rights of Children in Conflict with the Law".Geveva:*University of Fribourg

Dhungana, S. K. (2006a).*Impact of conflict on service delivery in rural Nepal: The case of health sector.* Paper presented at the international Conference on Governance and Development, Kandy, Sri Lanka, 16-19 August 2006.Education Journalists Group, Nepal.

Flesh trade on the rise due to increase in violence. (2004, 18 May). *The Kathmandu Post*

International Committee of the Red Cross.(2009) .*Families of missing persons in Nepal's study of their needs. Kathmandu:* Author

Joshi, A (n.d) *Impact of Armed Conflict on Children in Nepal: Situational Analysis of their health status* retrieved from

http://www.ksl.edu.np/kslcrc/articles/impact_of_armed_conflict_aruna.pdf on 6 June 2013

Joshi, A. (n.d) .*Impact of Armed Conflict on Children in Nepal: Situational Analysis of their health status.*Kathmandu: School of Law Child Rights Center, Nepal

Joshi, U &Paudel, R. (2006).*Pilot research on internal displacement due to armed conflict in Dhanusha district.* Kathmandu: National Human Rights Organization.Kathmandu: Friends for Peace. Pp 27-54.Kathmandu: Search for Common Ground Nepal.

Kumar, D. &Sharma, H. (2005).*Security Sector Reform in Nepal: Challenges and Opportunities.* Kathmandu: Friends for Peace.

Migration of Nepali children to India in the context of Nepal's armed conflict. Kathmandu.AuthorNepal: Left perspectives. New Delhi: Adroit.

Neupane, G. (2003). *The Maoist movement in Nepal:* A class perspective. In The people's war in

Pauletto, E., & Patel, P.(2010). Challenging child soldier DDR processes and policies in the Eastern Democratic Republic of Congo.*Journal of Peace, Conflict and Development,* 16, 35-57. Retrieved from http://www.bradford.ac.uk/ssis/peace-conflict-and-development/issue-16/childsoldiercongo.pdf

Pedersen, J., &Sommerfelt, T. (2007). Studying children in armed conflict: Data production, social indicators and analysis.*Social Indicators Research, 84*(3), 251-269. Retrieved from http://www.jstor.org/stable/pdfplus/10.2307/20734521.pdf?acceptTC=true

Pherali T.J. (2011) *Education and conflict in Nepal: possibilities for reconstruction* .Retrieved from http://www.informaworld.com/terms-and-conditions-of-access.pdf on 9 June 2013

Pherali, T.J. (2007). *The role of youth in peace building and community decision-making.*

Pyakurel, S. (2006). *'Kranti' ra 'Shanti' kochyapomamanabadhikar [Human rights in between]*

Roka.H.(2005). *Nepal-India border regulation in the context of present conflict.*

Save the Children Alliance&Central Child Welfare Board .(2005). *An increasing wave.*

Shakya, A. (2006).*Social Impact of Armed Conflict Nepal: Cause and Impact.*kathmandu: Social

   Inclusion Research Fund (SIRF)

Sharma, R. & B. Khadka. (2006*). Impact of armed conflict in education.* Kathmandu:

Sharma, S. (2006) .The Maoist Movement: An Evolutionary Perspective: *Himalayan 'People's*

War': Nepal's Maoist Rebellion. New Delhi: Foundations Books.

Shrestha ,B.&Niraula,S. (2005). *Internally Displaced Persons in Nepal. Peace and Democracy*

*in South Asia.*Kathmandu:1(2).

Shrestha, S. (2004) .*Impact of Armed Conflict on Children in Nepal*, web article dated

   21/07/2004, last updated 30/09/2004, visited on 25th Feb. 2014

Thapa, D. & B. Sijapati. (2004). *A kingdom under siege: Nepal's Maoist insurgency, 1996 to*

the rebellion and peace]. HimalKhabarpatrika, February 13_27, 55.

UNESCO International Bureau of Education (2004) *Education, conflict and social*

   cohesion.Retrived from http://www.ibe.unesco.org/en/conflict-social-cohesion/education-

   conflict-and-social-cohesion.html

Upreti, B. R. (2004). *The Price of Neglect: From Resource Conflict to Maoists Insurgency in the*

   Himalayan Kingdom. Kathmandu: Bhrikuti Academic Publications

Upreti, B. R. (2006). *Armed Conflict and Peace Process in Nepal: The Maoists Insurgency, Past*

   Negotiations and Opportunities for Conflict Transformation. Delhi: Adroit Publishers.

Vaux, T. Smith,A&Subba,S.(2006).*Education for All – Nepal Review from a conflict perspective.*Kathmandu:Author.

Wessells, M. (2005).Child soldiers, peace education, and postconflict reconstruction for peace.*Theory into Practice, 44*(4), 363-369. Retrieved from http://www.jstor.org/stable/pdfplus/10.2307/3496980.pdf

Annex:1.Number of killed Children

Table 1: *Human Consequences of Nepal's Armed Conflict*

Condition	Number by Maoist	Number by State	Total
Killed	4930	8339	13270
Children Killed (Below 17 yrs)	172	175	347
Disappeared	-	1147	1147

Source: Informal Sector Service Centre (INSEC), Oct 2006

Annex:2. Disappearance of students

Development region	Number of students disappeared (by state)	% of disappearance (by state)	Number of students disappeare d by rebels	% of disappearanc e by rebels
Eastern region	1	7.69	0	0
Central region	12	92.31	3,640	63.68
Western region	0	0	2,o75	36.30
Mid-western	0	0	1	0.02
Far-western *	0	0	0	0
Total		100	99.77	100

Sourse: Pherali (2011)